IT GETS DARK SO SOON NOW

It Gets Dark

So Soon Now

Poems

Kenneth Pobo

BROKEN TRIBE PRESS

It Gets Dark So Soon Now
Copyright © 2025 Kenneth Pobo
First Edition

Paperback ISBN: 9781965412176

Cover art: "On the horizon, the Angel of Certitude, and in the somber heaven a questioning eye." By Odilon Redon, 1882

Cover design by Jacob Arms

Published by Broken Tribe Press
Lawrence Landing Company
Raleigh, North Carolina 27609
USA, North America

Broken Tribe Press is a proud member of:

Independent Book Publishers Association
  and
Community of Literary Magazines and Presses

www.brokentribepress.com

CONTENTS

Rainbow Shirt

Red Lights

Porches And Shelves

For Stan

ACKNOWLEDGEMENTS

Thanks to the following editors of magazines who published work from this collection:

"Rainbow Shirt" *Bluepepper* (Australia)
"A Little Over 6000 Years Ago" Jambu Press: *Light On The Walls Of Life*
"My Invisible Friend" *Conch.es*
"I Say I'm 13" *The Waxed Lemon* (Ireland)
"At Home, Age 14, Radio On" *Trinity Review*
"Growing Up Gay In Villa Park, Illinois, 1968" Fauxmoir
"Tapioca" *Backwards Trajectory*
"The Summer I Listened To "Sugar Sugar" A Whole Lot" *Fieldstone Review* (Canada)
"When Tommy James Sang "Ball Of Fire"" *Verse-Virtual*
"Dear Eydie Gorme" *Dear*
"Note To Ethel Merman" *Cyclamen & Swords*
"It Gets Dark So Soon Now" *Washington Square Review*
"Pardon Me, But" *orangepeel*
"Laundromat Chat" *Agapanthus*
"Beyond The Suburb" *Portland Metrozine*
"Leaky Love Affair" *The Rumen*
"Aim, Fire" *The Camel's Saloon*
"In Tupperware" *Delicate Friend*
"Let Go" *Medicinal Purposes*
"Someone On A Train" *In Parentheses*
"1,2,3 Red Light" *Rat's Ass Review*
"Kingda Ka" *The Alembic*
"While Driving To Work" *Moonlighting*
"About Him," *Local Train*
"We're Not In Kansas Anymore" *Chiron Review*
"Dorothy Back In The Emerald City" *Poesy*
"Made For Walkin'" *Champagne Room*

"Pandora And I Do Dishes Together" *And The Men Came And Danced* (anthology)
"Lunch At The Radisson Hotel" *Gopherwood Review*
"We Can't" *The Paradox Magazine*
"Baseball Scoring" Blood Pudding Press
"Sad Guitar" *American Journal of Poetry*
"Red Guitar" *Seventh Quarry*
"This Lover I Had" *Penumbra*
"Naked Lunch" *Juice*
"Michael With The Tired Arms" *American Journal of Poetry*
"Waiting For Rain" *Melting Trees Review*
"On Our Porch" *Home Planet News*
"Gladly Stolen" *The Mark Review*
"My Baby Does The Hanky Panky" *Old Hickory Review*
"The Honeymooners" *The Bombay Literary Magazine*
"Dark Castle?" *Edgar*
"While You Shelve" *Iddie*
"While You Hack" *Passager*
"Happy Trails" *Velvet Avalanche Poetry Anthology*
"Fernando Drops By" *Darling, Can You Hear Me*
"Thirty Years" *Shadowplay*
"Wedding Day" *Local Train*
"After A Moderate Fight" *Alternate Route*
"Anniversary for Old Dudes" *The Journal* (United Kingdom)

Rainbow Shirt

RAINBOW SHIRT

I sit in my rainbow shirt.
A stranger tells me
to burn it. The bumpy
bus craves the anonymous.
We're nobody
to each other.
He looks at me like
he might puke.

Well, dude, go ahead.
The shirt can be washed.
The rainbow withstands
the storm.

A GOLD LIGHT

Sometimes
I find a gold
light that bursts
from a dark cave.
I bask in it,
begin my day.

A LITTLE OVER 6000 YEARS AGO

"And give us new dreams to dream,
Give us new myths to live by!"
     —Lawrence Ferlinghetti, "To the Oracle at Delphi"

Adam pops out
from behind a crabapple tree,
in bloom of course, everything
always blooming. Nothing dies.
He says he wants to have sex

which will be perfect because
he's perfect, I'm perfect,
and we'll both enjoy it perfectly
before we eat perfect food
that God provides. It's tasty,
but I get a yen for forbidden fruit--

I'll bet it's perfect too. I pick some
and hand it to Adam who takes it
perfectly well. Oh my, we're naked.
Hc sees this too. Our imperfections
run under ferns like mice.
God is angry and perfect.
After we get expelled, Adam wants

sex again. He doesn't even ask.
He's the only game in town. I wish
God would quit watching us.
We have discovered privacy.

MY INVISIBLE FRIEND

Dun Dunt knew many things.
He still knows many things
but keeps most of them
to himself. He's like a cave

full of treasure. Spelunking
gets tiring as I retrieve
heavy nuggets--I need them
to build my life.

I SAY I'M 13

Our homeroom teacher tries
to make sure we are all where
we're supposed to be,
section 12. I'm never where
I'm supposed to be. Supposed
is a word like rutabaga.
I dislike both. I think
she's asking for our ages
so I say 13.

The class is full of pigs
who escaped the pen.
Oinkers fly out
the classroom windows,
rest on clouds, snuffle and drool—
maybe they're supposed to be
on clouds and I'm supposed
to be diagramming a sentence
that takes me hostage
and smothers me
with an angry adjective.

AT HOME, AGE FOURTEEN, RADIO ON

I kept it to myself.
It felt worse to admit
to anyone,
even my parents.

Bullies take your tongue
when they attack, demand
silence. At least I had

music, bubblegum songs,
The 1910 Fruitgum Company
and The Ohio Express.
Even today, the porch quiet
and cats asleep,
tunes ripple through me—

peace comes,
a red dahlia
against a gray sky.

GROWING UP GAY
IN VILLA PARK, ILLINOIS, 1968

I couldn't let the other kids know.
Teachers? No thanks.
"Nixon's The One" on their bumpers.

In church I had the right smile.

Villa Avenue, lined with Dutch Elm trees,
a leafy canopy over commuters
in cars and kids riding bicycles.

Prom? I wanted to invite Troy.
He didn't want to be shoved
in a locker upside down.

I tried to hide
in every sidewalk crack.
Hiding gets dangerous.
You can die from it.
And no one would even know.

TAPIOCA

When my dad bowls on Monday night,
mom sets up the card table so
we can eat dinner with The Monkees.
I have a crush on Mike. It's the wool hat,
elan for a seventh grader.

WCFL plays "Tapioca Tundra."
The lyrics make no sense
so I'm drawn to them. In English
we write about hidden meanings.
I don't like when meanings hide
though I hide too,
a Monkees boy
in a Blind Faith world. I like tapioca

and gym is my tundra where it's
always cold. The song begins
to make sense when little else does.

THE SUMMER I LISTENED TO "SUGAR, SUGAR" BY THE ARCHIES A WHOLE LOT

At almost fifteen, I felt
that I was floating
in an air balloon
over Villa Park—the fire
went out and I began to sink.
Clouds that seemed friendly
now looked like paid assassins.

One way to relight the fire
and prevent a crash was to listen
to music, the bubblegummier
the better. The Archies took over
the radio with a song so sweet
it could give you cavities. I wasn't
in love then, just waking up to it,
scared, preferring a longer air

balloon ride. The Archies
brought me down safely. Love
wouldn't be as gentle.

WHEN TOMMY JAMES SANG
"BALL OF FIRE"

in 1969, I was 15, optimistic
despite body bags served with supper.
We had recently walked on the moon.
I was part

of that we. Earth
felt like everyone had a share
just as we had the same moon
to fall in love under.
My rose-colored glasses could turn
any kaleidoscope color

or so I thought. At 62
I'm kidney stones and white hair
on the barber's sheet. America
a front for the KKK. I suppose
rose-colored glasses had to
go smash. I couldn't see well
through them anyway, hadn't expected
glass shards in my eyes.

Songs of peace
and love
joined the NRA,
the ball of fire, nuclear,
looking for a place to fall.

ROPE

In college gym, Coach made me
climb the rope.
This was not possible
with my soft arms.

When my turn came, I stayed
on the floor, got no lift off.
The other guys looked at me
like of course he can't do it—
dumb faggot. Some ropes

I never got tested on,
like can I climb high enough
over insults, the needle words
that sewed me into silence?
I did get to the top of that rope.

They never saw.
They weren't looking.
They chased footballs,
the cobra ropes ready to strike.

DEAR EYDIE GORME,

My husband is out of town,
and in our messy house
I fret about cat hair.
It's everywhere, much of it
threading my brain. I'm lonely
as a plastic bottle of sparkling water
waiting for a hand. I don't expect
my husband to ease my loneliness.
He can, but I can be lonely anywhere.
Once I broke down weeping in
a swanky elevator. I get out

my records and find "Tonight I'll
Say A Prayer," which brought you back
to the Hot 100 in late 1969. At fifteen
I didn't much like that year despite
some faded hilarity. The song
is yearning which I do well.
If my yearns were gasoline, many trucks
could crisscross the country from them.

Night takes menacing steps into
the living room. With no defense,
I turn you up louder. Tonight
I'll say a prayer. Grab it for me
and send it to a dahlia just coming into
bloom on heaven's weedy outskirts.

NOTE TO ETHEL MERMAN

Ethel, everything may be coming
up roses, but remember
that roses have thorns
to poke your eye out,
and they draw Japanese beetles
eating small holes in petals,
turning stem into desert,
and they often get black spot,
can defoliate completely.

My gym buddy says,
"Roses will break your heart."
If everything is coming
up roses, prepare for the worst.
And best.

IT GETS DARK SO FAST NOW

The end of the year, a car
with a bad battery. When you try
to start it you hear a weary
whirr, then nothing. You know
you should've taken care of this
months ago. You kept watching
Downton Abbey, wishing that
you too could wear cool clothes.
The sun steps out of the room
more and more. You look
for the light switch. It hides.

You think of death. First
you eat a sugar cookie. Next
you imagine a cemetery
on a freezing day, your body
getting lowered. People
at the gravesite smell whiskey.
You welcome worms.
You have no other choice.

SILENCE IS LAVENDER

Odin rumbles down
from lavender skies and says
he has much to say
that we need to hear. We await
his words, but he stays
silent. That's his message,
I guess. Don't always speak.
Wear a lavender wind
and blow through local trees.
When he's ready to return
to Valhalla, we say go ahead,
but please leave a lavender
footprint in our lavender yard.

STONEWALL RIOTS

Many of us thought
we were "different,"
a polite way
to say gay,
a polite way
to not say.

At 14, the Sunday
after Stonewall,
a red hymnal
on my lap,
I was there
and not there.
We sang
"Trust And Obey"

with little reason
to trust, even less
to obey.

WHY SO RESPECTFUL?

At 18 I was still attending
the Bible Church, a sad gathering
of thirty or forty people
who believed in rewards
and punishments. Truth
wore dowdy clothes. Most
of the Bibles wore black.

Our minister, who saw me reading
Psychology Today in the town
library, asked if this magazine
in any way honored God.
I wish now, half a century later,
I had vomited all over him.
Instead I said I was doing research
for a class. Always the evasion,

always being put in a position
where evasion seems safest.
Until you see you've been
evading yourself.

PARDON ME, BUT

do you see us here,
in the living room, drinking
a mimosa? I think we're visible,
but maybe not. This must be
another don't ask
don't tell family.
Only we told.

It's not disapproval, exactly,
while your discomfort
removes our skin,
who we are.
Everything is so nice,
table surfaces shining,
windows washed,
a middle-class Grand Canyon.
We can yell but sound disappears.

In plain sight our bodies
fade into couch cushions,
an indoor fog.

LAUNDROMAT CHAT

Katie and I often do laundry
at the same time. She says that laundry
will be her death while filling
a front loader. Her husband would
let the clothes stink until he couldn't
go to work. Even then. She knows
that I'm gay since my underwear
told her behind my back. I tell her
about my husband who likes to say
I'll get to it. She says I'm lucky
that I don't have kids. They outgrow
everything except requests.

Our clothes dislike both of us.
I can't blame them. I wouldn't
want to be fed detergent
and stuffed into a machine either.
After we fold and trap them
in a box, we drive home.

BEYOND THE SUBURB

I first watched it when I was a high school sophomore, home with the flu, feeling better but still weak. Mom put a silver pail down by the couch "in case you need to puke, use this." I did need to puke when I got up, but that was hours before. She grabbed the pail and flushed the puke. She sat in the dining room in her usual chair under the cuckoo clock with the annoying red bird that popped out and read her Devotions. She took me to church many times, but it didn't take.

The film was *Beyond The Forest* from 1949. I hadn't come out myself yet. I got together with Tom Konwitz for what he called "fun." It was fun. I looked forward to those times. He said "It's just something to do."

Bette Davis, wearing a strange black fright wig, was Rosa Moline: "a twelve o'clock girl in a nine o'clock town." Drab as a fence post husband Joseph Cotton, oh so very good, oh so unappreciated—in a town no one wants to visit. Bette plotted to escape. Maybe a rich Chicago dude would make her rich, offer her the gift of excitement. Other than my romps with Tom, not much got exciting in Gradyville. Philadelphia was fairly nearby, but I didn't take the train in much. My dad said, "You're such a scatterbrain, you'll lose your wallet, and I'll have to come get you, and you know I won't be happy about that."

That dullard friend of her achingly good Cotton, Moose, who she, oops, kills, said "You're one for the birds, Rosa, one for the birds." I, too, was for the birds. I waited for bluebirds to return in spring, hung a picture of a snowy owl on my bedroom wall that looked like Peggy Lee.

Of course I got better and high school roped me back in and covered me in geometry. I had gotten beyond the suburb. I didn't want a saccharine doctor to house me or a small town or suburb to keep me in one form of high school after another. I knew I'd leave. Mom's cuckoo clock bird kept returning to the clock's innards. Maybe it would be a city. Maybe not. My time to fly kept getting closer.

LEAKY LOVE AFFAIR

You said you'd love me the way
a roof loves the garage it covers.
As a roof, are you leaky
or sealed? Sometimes
I wish my garage had no roof,
a better way to see
hummingbirds. Or clouds
doing ballet practice.

We could sit among rakes,
wipe our hands with oily rags
and watch the first snowfall.

You wouldn't need to be a roof.
I like skin.
Sit close to me.

ICEBREAKER

At the conference I draw
a folded blue paper that says
describe my sex life.
I'm game. These writers wear
provocative hats. One told
a funny story about her big toe. So,

my sex life is "Crimson And Clover"
by Tommy James and the Shondells.
My sex life is a goddess on a first date.
My sex life is a vowel-y word
like onomatopoeia. My sex life
hopes the elevator gets stuck
between floors. My sex life makes
a tulip blush which coaxes
the rest of the garden to bloom.
My sex life, an owl on top
of a dumpster, asks who. And
my sex life is corn on the cob,
butter drippy, my mouth
greasy and warm.

AIM, FIRE

When Tom says,
You're a dick!
and I get huffy,
he says nobody means anything
by it, I'm too sensitive.

I claim that I'm not
a dick,
that I'm a warm wool blanket
of a man. I say he's
too sensitive. Toaster-coil

red, he says *You really are
a bitch*, spits the word out
like bitter coffee. If
a word could be a gun,

he'd load and fire it
directly in my face.

IN TUPPERWARE

In my county, we put our genitals
in Tupperware, find a spot
in the back of the fridge's
bottom shelf, and say I really
should clean out the fridge
someday. My neighbor

holds a Tupperware party. Guests
bring Tupperware containers.
All I have are my genitals.
When people see them,
each says they have them too.

I may stop storing them
in the fridge. No more secrets
between my legs. Tonight's yellow
moon is a McDonald's fry
bent down to see if I'm naked.
I eat the moon,
and call some stars for strip poker.

SOMEONE ON A TRAIN TOLD ME

that I shouldn't use the word "lovely."
Men shouldn't use words like that.
It makes them sound effeminate.
It makes them sound, well,
you know. I had been talking
to my friend about my new
Neil Diamond rose with lovely
blossoms. Maybe I should
have said the blossoms were bullets.
He might have preferred that.
He lacked a lovely face. Strange
blobs of hate dripped
from his forehead down his neck.
He went back to his screen,
hunched down between clicks,
got off at Elwyn Station--so far
I've never seen him again.
Lovely.

LET GO!

I don't fret summer's death.
True, my snapdragons drop,
and by late November
even the Helen Traubel
rose peters out. In fall

I hold things too tight,
add piles to piles--how
to let wind blow leaves away,
me not chasing after.

Grab hold, let go, grab hold,
let go, let go, let go,
like the maple who turns
grass gold
and red
setting each leaf free.

(haiku)

When a haiku comes
out of the closet, every
syllable dances.

Red Lights

"1,2,3 Red Light"

God the stop light,
the don't, the you'll be sorry if you do.

I wait for the light to change
while you say let's get naked
behind the paint store
where no one goes after closing,
only a short drive. The signal
changes three times
and I don't go until
someone honks. I head
to the paint store,
where we see green ferns

and green grass, the red sun
setting behind a yellow jalopy.

KINGDA KA

Jeff and Jerry drive to the courthouse
and say I do.

Marriage,
the Kingda Ka coaster,
New Jersey everywhere you look,
zero to 128 mph.
Three and a half seconds. A kiss

takes off, breaks apart
by a cookie jar.

WHILE DRIVING TO WORK

In the car "Could It Be Forever"
by David Cassidy came on,
a 1972 hit, and—that's when
the only being I told
I was gay to was God. My prayers
were please help me be
sexually drawn to women. OK,
I didn't say sexually. I said
romantically. This was God.
I felt I had to be polite,
at least discreet, figuring
that God would get it anyway.

I wondered about forever love.
The Beatles sang that all
I needed was love. Why
was I fenced out?
Until,

five years later when I
quit asking God for help,
kicked down the fence,
turned pickets into firewood,
and sat by the blaze.

ABOUT HIM

In school Harold Cockring Fizzlebotts
drew horses with enormous penises.
I said I liked squirrels.

He said someday he'd be a king
with a flaming gold crown.
Kings seemed like teachers
or our minister, George Crayhorn,
who, at 28, had apparently slept with
my mother, said adultery was wrong,
but he knew God
so just be chill.

Harold Cockring Fizzlebotts didn't attend
any church. His invisible horse
took him to an invisible throne.
Invisible people worshipped him.
He needed help. We poked at our phones.

He turned into a stack of rumors.
Did he die? Was he in porn?
Did he run a far-right website?
Perhaps he's a broken window,
sunlight through shards,
making a dark room visible.

WE'RE NOT IN KANSAS,
WE'RE NOT IN PENNSYLVANIA,
WE'RE NOT ANYWHERE ANYMORE

A man enters a mall,
buys a PEACE shirt.
Security arrests him. Such
a crime can cost a year
in jail. A guy

on a Santa Fe library computer
joins a chat room, says,
"Trump is out of control."
Authorities get him,
quiz him for five hours.

On TV, the War is a Holy
Communion of bomb
and blast. Commentators
masturbate
right in front of everyone,
cum over every
White House word,

insist we cum too. *Life*?
Count the body bags.
Liberty? The attorney general
cancelled it. *Pursuit of happiness*? We are
being pursued-- cut your lights.
They keep looking in.

DOROTHY BACK IN THE EMERALD CITY

While ironing clothes, the son
of the son of the son
of Toto circles her. Cloud
witches wave. Busted bike
wheels turn. A smell of apple

cake wafts from a window. She
remembers Emerald City--
three pals who no longer rule,
took jobs in better kingdoms.
Scarecrow an adjunct
professor. Tinman a gardener.
Lion an army meteorologist.
She's mostly forgotten.

Digital clocks replaced
the hour glass which held
Auntie Em's face. She'd stay
if she could, cling to color.
She kicks a broken fan
in her prairie house,
barometer falling--a seesaw
wind whirls, storm near.

MADE FOR WALKIN'

I'm wearing my glam
glitter boots and walking
up to Wawa to buy
a warm pretzel. This is risky.

As a man, I'm supposed to be
a colorless pebble under
a creek. My shoes,
which I've read are the first things
that people notice, must be black
or maybe brown. Those shoes
remind me of the hushpuppies
my geometry teacher wore.
What a bore to hand your life
over to proving that a triangle
is a triangle. I'll take its word for it.

These ruby red shoes,
Dorothy in a disco,
looking for a home.
I have a home—that cloud,
almost dispersing,
unveiling blue sky.

PANDORA AND I DO DISHES TOGETHER

She has traveled high
mountains between centuries
to enter a kitchen

with a dirty floor. She's careful
with each dish,
even if they're hot

and slippery. If I don't
clean one perfectly, she
hands it back. My husband

and I have a room for her.
She can sleep anywhere,
even inside a grain of sand.

When I clumsily break
a cranberry red juice glass,
she runs out into the yard,

calls to a crow
to take her away,
her feathered taxi.

LUNCH AT THE RADISSON, 1987

"How will I recognize you?"
"I'll wear a gray jacket,"

our clothes, telegraph
blips, stoplights.

Flirtatious over orange juice,
our anecdotes click

against salt and pepper shakers.
Am I

your type? Do I
sound forced?

Coffee after lunch. Sex
pours our water--are you

safe? What do you do
in bed? This leads us

into the country
of Death. Our brothers

are here, dead,
but with us like lungs.

In the empty parking lot
we don't kiss goodbye.

Death watches
from a safe distance.

WE CAN'T

My brother Ralph tells me
that I have it easy since TV
now has shows like
Queer Eye for the Straight Guy
and why must I always talk

about being gay? I rarely
bring it up, but it is who I am.
Of course he rambles on about
his failed relationship with Donna.
I like Donna. I like Ralph too
when he shows me the Ingraham
Mantel Clock that he made
work like new. I'm all thumbs.
We can't

really talk. It's like we're on
opposite sides of a lake shouting
at each other. Or we're lost
in a cave, the darkness so deep
that we lose each other.

BASEBALL SCORING

In junior high I heard about getting
on base with girls, knew
guys wanted me to hit
homers. A field, the girl
controlled how far we got.
She couldn't hit, run
or walk.

If I were going to score,
I wanted it to be with boys—
the eighth-grade rulebook
provided no lingo.

First base? Copping a feel of
a locker room butt.
Second base? Kissing
in the field behind school.
Third base? Jerking together.
<u>*A homer*</u>? A dick in a male mouth
or ass.

I wasn't ready to slam homers,
didn't want to score,
find it's only a game.

Someone has to lose.

SAVED

At Scripture Press, mom bought
devotionals. I found a pamphlet,
The Gay Blade. This gay guy
found Jesus who dressed him
in a blue suit and voila,
no need to think pink.
Be blue. Marry,
have kids, go to church.
You'll all die
and meet up in heaven,
blue as can be.

Had I met the gay blade
I'd have asked him if he wanted
to get a Coke. We could talk.

Who knows?
A life, two lives,
could be saved.

SAD GUITAR

Our friend Jose told me
love drove him
crazy.

It's true.

He lives in our cupboard
behind tea cups,
plays a sad guitar
that cracks
the butter dish,
shards among
mouse turds.

RED GUITAR

A guitar lets me travel
across any continent--

despite my warbly voice,
I sing. Notes pour out, and,

like kids, they dance
without knowing any steps.

THIS LOVER I HAD

claimed to be from New Brunswick,
but when I absently asked what its
capital was, he went blank
as a manikin. I decided he was just

geographically challenged until
he called New Brunswick his favorite state—
crocked on vodka, he admitted
he was from Abilene but didn't sound

like any Texan I knew. We parted irritably.
From now on I'm going to ask all
potential lovers to take a 30-minute test:
history, geography, even a short writing sample.

It probably won't help. Lies perform
acrobatic tricks right in my living room.
As I applaud, they are already
stealing the bric-a-brac.

MICHAEL WITH THE TIRED ARMS

Michael, stop your rowing,
at least for a few moments.
You want to get to shore,
beat out a possible storm.

What's there that makes you
want to arrive so much?
Nordstrom's? A Sears
that closed and in the parking lot
dealers sell opioids? Let
our boat drift and you'll see a loon
diving underwater, a bird cork
popping up thirty feet away.
Or a stand of pines where
an eagle nests. We could
watch her swoop down for a fish.

You work too hard. The seducer
shore offers little love.
  Drift.
    Float.
      A water lily
will recommend you
to that early pink vein of dusk.

NAKED LUNCH

Naked   bleeding   half blind   is
   this where taxis dump   dead
        pedestrians   maybe
     I'm in a condom   swimming in

            a stranger's jism   or this
            is the real hell   a table   kids
         whining about shoes   dad bitching
         about cooked carrots   mom pissing
         her troubles on The View   my skin

            a cabinet full of   knives
             they open   all the time   take
             what they need   go   tomorrow
                  bag lady   dead behind Wal-Mart
holding a Wendy's   paper cup

Porches And Shelves

WAITING FOR RAIN AFTER HOT DAYS

The sky is like a gray hill.
I can easily climb to the top—
when the rain falls, I'll grab
a raindrop and fall
back to the ground. I love

when Jay and the Americans sing
"Walkin' in the Rain."
Such a good idea! I walk and walk,
take off my shirt, let the storm
get familiar with my shoulders,
kiss rivers
forming on my lips. My husband

opens a window and yells
that I should come out of the rain.
I yell that he should join me.

The sun will rise over the hill.
Too soon.
Then I'll go back in.

ON OUR PORCH

You say it hurts to see
the tree behind our garden bed
turn yellow. It's too soon,
autumn knocking at our door.

Back home, my family had
a Chinese elm that sometimes
called fall in early. A prophesy,
the days of school way too near.
I thought that tree would
never die. Also thought
that I'd spend my days
in Washington School forever,
writing book reports
on Sunday afternoons until

I turned ninety. An ice storm
killed the tree. I grew up and got
a degree in confusion. Today,
yellow leaves increase.
I feel them falling inside me.

GLADLY STOLEN

How can love be stolen?
It's not like a pie
when the thief comes by
and grabs it when the widow
is downstairs pulling laundry
from the dryer—or

is it? You stole me
from my life of everyday
will be like everyday until I die.
I hadn't locked up my heart—

you took it and ran. Maybe

I stole yours too. You said
you thought of your life then
as a tip left on a table.
I scooped up the dough
and said let's go. Out for pie.
Which we did, red cherries
and a flaky crust. It still is,

27 years later,
warm from the oven,
ice cream melting on top.

I CAN'T HELP MYSELF

No one has called me sugar pie
or honeybunch. On the night
when I met my husband,
the black gumball sky spilled
from a moonless machine.
We had no pet names.

I can't help myself when
we kiss. It's like being
let into the Emerald City
only no wizard gives orders.
Horses change color and
the pre-kiss world huddles
among printers and passwords.

Magic starts to snow
even though it is still warm.

MY BABY DOES THE HANKY PANKY

You are full of moons and stars
and all that stuff. Look,
I can only offer you undying
love and eternal devotion
(I must be mad!)—surely
that's enough. Oh, I see,
only worship will do. You're
God and I'm a tidy woman
knitting Heaven with a rosary.

I really love the way you do
the hanky panky—you've been
dancing alone, scared
I'll be like the others.

I may be. We betray each other
the way leaves betray trunks.
That's no excuse, but
what are you going to do?
Be alone? It's safe that way,
maybe. Frogs understand this too—
in green ponds, singing
repetitive songs.

THE HONEYMOONERS

When I married Stan, we
honeymooned on Triton, a lovely
hotel built from frozen nitrogen. Oh,
that was grand. 235 degrees
below zero made us cling tightly.

Lonely Neptune captured Triton.
It worked out well for everyone.

Stan and I plan a second honeymoon.
This time we'll jump on a methane
ice trampoline, hold each other
with every leap, kiss in mid-air
the way Nereid and Naiad do
when our telescopes have
gone to sleep.

DARK CASTLE?

Castles may have webs
and look messy, but go
in most any room, stand
under any portrait with its eyes

cut out so ghosts can
watch you, and the whole
shebang's one big spark--
centuries live there, years

that outburn any fire.
When people say, oow,
look out, that castle, it's so
dark... are they imagining

their own electric houses
with glowing appliances?
O terrible darkness, you'll
never get me in one of those!

MY HUSBAND DOESN'T NEED WINGS

While we're getting ready
to watch *Jeopardy* and maybe
Wheel of Fortune, he opens
the window—and flies out,
makes it over the maple
and down Lund Lane.
When he returns we talk
about his first flight.
Would he keep flying? Yes,
he thinks he will.
And he does.

I accept it. The way I accept
the coming of dusk.
Or death.
Or the coming of death.

WHILE YOU SHELVE

records, upstairs I sort laundry. Socks,
you can pick out yours,

I can't. I visit with the pomegranate's
three reddish-orange blossoms, fire

against glass. The pitcher plant,
an all-night diner, no customers—

it took eleven years to find one house.
By spring, clothes flapping on a line,

maybe our sorting will be easier,
windows open, bulbs up.

WHILE YOU HACK

and hack, unable to sleep,
I talk to the oleander I dug up
in early November and placed on
the bay window. If I blast

The Dave Clark 5,
she lolls in sunlight,
her way of humming. Music,
your hacking upstairs,

it's all the same to this plant
who tells me her recurring
dream of light
yellow blossoms, a red

brick wall nearby, and bees bringing
hive gossip each day until
buoyant buzzing quiets,
stalk leaning to the light.

HAPPY TRAILS

13 years ago, we'd rub
our dicks all over each
other's bellies till we came
and collapsed. Glorious!

Now we're either oral
or anal. Let's go back,
let our dicks lead the way,
play as we did before,

open, hungry, moist
and grooved with hot
cum jets
on our happy trails.

FERNANDO DROPS BY

looking both gaunt and dapper.
He's my friend--we go back
centuries. In the Civil War,

he and I were lovers. I surrendered
to him long before Appomattox.
In World War One he became a bluebird

flying over trenches and latrines,
never getting shot down. We've
had fights. He can sting not like a bee

but like the smell of a nasty cheese.
Maybe a few more centuries will help us
to better understand each other.

Or not. Understanding might
not be needed. I didn't understand
his white jump suits but liked

to see him wear them. He didn't
understand when I told him I was really
Nina, a ballerina. Years passed

and tea made itself in the dark.
Fireflies wrote important books
they read by their own light.

THIRTY YEARS

On a cold sunny day, we got married.
The Unitarian Church held much light.
The minister was gracious and polite.
He didn't question us about our creed.
Some churches refused us despite our need.
We celebrated with our friends that night.
On a cold sunny day, love kept us warm.

We turned away fears so that we felt freed.
After twenty-five years, we felt no fright.
The moon popped in for sheet cake, wearing white.
Sometimes love grows from the tiniest seed.
On a cold sunny day, no threat of storm.

WEDDING DAY

January 13, 2017

Our road had no markers,
no signs to give us directions.
Yet we got on it anyway, hoping
that the sky would provide light
before we hit potholes
and broke down. Often

we doubted that we'd make it,
yet the touch of a hand,
quiet moments shared
in a midnight house, helped us
to see orchids hidden
behind darkness, an almost
crazy belief that we'd find our way

here, today, with family
and friends, two cats waiting
at home, ears up,
our road always
leading us home.

AFTER A MODERATE FIGHT

On our wedding day, the gray sky
offered some bright sunny moments.
When we have a fight, I think of
clouds that break up before they fly
away. I sink into silence,
mourn the possible loss of love.
We make up. Somehow. Everything
feels right despite a shallow sting.

Our house holds joy—and some anger.
We're like two creeks joined together
or two frogs croaking and calling.
I guess love is about falling
and getting up again. Again.
Two clocks on one wall, two old men.

ANNIVERSARY FOR OLD DUDES

You told me you hated literature
because of high school and *The Great Gatsby*.
Mrs. Applewood, an angry teacher,
blathered on that symbolism was key.
All you wanted was to fix up your car
to drive you from T.J. Eckleburg's eyes.
The school bell, the slowest thing, a thick tar.
Pages trapped you in a book you despised.

When we met, you were in engineering,
a field I didn't understand. I wrote
poems about whatever I was fearing.
I wonder why we got on the same boat—
thirty years ago. It still stays afloat,
even when storms give it a battering.

ABOUT THE AUTHOR

Kenneth Pobo (he/him) lives in Pennsylvania. He is the author of twenty-one chapbooks and nine full-length collections. Recent books include *Bend of Quiet* (Blue Light Press), *Loplop in a Red City* (Circling Rivers), *Uneven Steven* (Assure Press), *Sore Points* (Finishing Line Press) *Lilac and Sawdust* (Meadowlark Press), *Lavender Fire, Lavender Rose* (BrickHouse Books) and *At The Window, Silence* (Fernwood Press). Human rights issues, especially as they relate to the LGBTQIA+ community, are also a constant presence in his work.

www.ingramcontent.com/pod-product-compliance
Lightning Source LLC
Chambersburg PA
CBHW031247120626
46545CB00007B/2687